# Wildlife In Your Backyard

## If You Care, Leave it There

Wildlife Haven Rehabilitation Centre

Published by Oak Island Publications
oakislandpublications@gmail.com

Published in Canada

First Printing, April 2016 by CreateSpace
Published by Wildlife Haven Rehabilitation Centre

ISBN-10: 152094824X
ISBN-13: 978-1530948246

# Acknowledgments

We would like to thank our staff and volunteers for their endless amount of dedication, caring for the animals, educating the public about wildlife and everything else in between.

# Dedications

This book is dedicated to our past, present and future non-releasable wildlife ambassadors that allow us to educate the public about the importance of wildlife, which we must respect and protect.

Winnipeg

Ile des Chênes

# Introduction

Since 1984, Wildlife Haven Rehabilitation Centre (WHRC) has rehabilitated more than 35,000 injured, sick and orphaned patients from all over Manitoba and Northwestern Ontario. Wildlife Haven is a volunteer-driven, registered charity dedicated to the rehabilitation of injured, sick and orphaned wildlife for their return back to the wild. WHRC provides educational services to the community and engages volunteers in a rewarding experience.

Wildlife Haven Rehabilitation Centre, originally known as Manitoba Wildlife Rehabilitation Organization (MWRO), was formed by a group of environmentally concerned citizens. The volunteers started the organization out of their backyards and the first Centre opened in 1993 in Glenlea, Manitoba. The Centre is now located in Ile des Chênes, Manitoba.

Wildlife Haven is provincially and federally permitted for wildlife rehabilitation. It adheres to the Wildlife Rehabilitators Code of Ethics and Minimum Standards for Wildlife Rehabilitation. These standards were developed by the National Wildlife Rehabilitators Association and the International Wildlife Rehabilitation Council with Certified Wildlife Rehabilitators. The organization's staff and volunteers attend education seminars and training events.

Wildlife Haven Rehabilitation Centre relies on the generous support of volunteers and donations to operate. More information can be found online at wildlifehaven.ca regarding the organization and wildlife rehabilitation.

# The Importance of Wildlife Rehabilitation

Wildlife rehabilitation is about treating and caring for injured, sick and orphaned wildlife for their return to the wild. It's about giving a second chance to the wild animals found in our backyards, in the park and throughout various habitats.

Wildlife patients are admitted to rehabilitation centres, such as Wildlife Haven for many reasons; from orphaned animals such as baby squirrels and baby birds who have lost their parents, to birds of prey that are hunting along roads and in ditches and get struck by vehicles. Sometimes patients are admitted due to natural reasons, just like when you get sick. Other times, wildlife are brought in because of human modification of the environment. Collisions with windows, getting struck by cars, and being electrocuted by power lines are only a few examples of the challenges that wildlife face in today's world. In both of these cases, the patients require medical attention, food and a safe place away from predators and other dangers to allow them to heal.

Fortunately, there are caring individuals who help these distressed animals find their way to rehabilitation centres to be cared for and rehabilitated. These centers often consult with concerned citizens and together allow healthy wildlife to remain in the wild where they belong.

**Red Squirrels**

## Squirrels

In the spring, orphaned Squirrels are often found alone and brought to Wildlife Haven. However, sometimes when you find a young Squirrel at the bottom of a tree, mom is close by and in the process of relocating their nest. To avoid unnecessary orphans, if the young squirrel is healthy, wait 24 hours to see if the mom will retrieve it before bringing it to our Centre.

**Northern Flying Squirrel**

**Fox Squirrel**

## Fun Facts

- Squirrels can find food buried beneath 30 cm of snow, the length of a ruler
- The front teeth of Squirrels never stop growing
- Squirrels build routes in their nests to escape predators

**Grey Squirrels**

# Rabbits & Hares

In the spring, Rabbits and Hares are often found injured, sick or orphaned. However, not all of them are true orphans. Many people are unaware that the mothers will only visit the young at dusk and dawn, to avoid attracting predators.

Eastern Cottontails

Eastern Cottontails

Snowshoe Hare

Eastern Cottontail

## Did you know...

- Hare babies are born fully furred with their eyes open
- Rabbit babies are born furless with their eyes closed
- Rabbits are independent when they are the size of a tennis ball

# Raccoons

Every spring, Wildlife Haven answers numerous calls about Raccoons. They are often found as pests in attics of houses. People will often trap the mother and unknowingly, leave the young behind. This results in unnecessary orphans that need to be raised at our Centre.

Wildlife Haven can provide advice on how to humanely encourage Raccoons to leave on their own.

# Fun Facts

- Raccoons have opposable thumbs, this means their hands are human-like

- Raccoons wash their food in rivers and streams before eating it

- Raccoons are scavengers and will eat almost anything, but they really enjoy crayfish

- Raccoons can make up to 51 different sounds

# Coyotes

Wildlife Haven received Coyote pups in the spring after spending three days orphaned in a farmer's field. At just a week old, they were in need of a special formula to match the nutrition they would receive from their mother's milk.

When they reached two months old, other foods were introduced into their diet to wean them off the formula. In the fall, when they had grown big and learned how to catch prey, they were released back to the wild.

# Did you know...

- Wean/weaning: the time when other foods replace mother's milk
- Coyotes communicate by scent-marking and group-howling
- Coyotes play an important role in maintaining the balance of animals in the environment

# Woodchucks

Woodchucks are the largest mammal that goes into true hibernation. They are often found as orphans and then admitted to our Centre. Once they are weaned they require their weight in greens every day, which is about 6 cups.

# Fun Facts

- True hibernation: when an animal's body temperature drops to nearly freezing and their heart beat slows down
- Woodchucks, often called Groundhogs, predict whether or not there will be six more weeks of winter or an early spring on February 2nd, Groundhog day

# Bobcat

An orphaned, female Bobcat was found in a woodpile in winter. She was about 2 months old, weak and starving. Once she arrived at Wildlife Haven she was rehydrated and provided with food to regain her strength. After caring for her for 7 months, she was successfully released back into the wild.

## Did you know...

- The Bobcat's main source of food is rabbits and hares
- The Bobcat is about double the size of an average house cat
- Bobcats are solitary animals

## Fun Facts

- The Bobcat's growls and snarls are very deep and often sound as if they are coming from a larger animal

- Bobcats can pounce a distance of 3 meters, the height of a basketball net

- The Bobcat is named after its short, bobbed tail

- Bobcats can climb and swim

- Bobcats are most active at dawn and dusk

**Blue Jay & American Robins**

**Bohemian Waxwing**

**Common Grackles**

# Songbirds

Many Songbird species can be found in Manitoba. Wildlife Haven often cares for Rock Doves, Sparrows and Robins. In the spring, many baby birds that have fallen out of their nests are admitted for care. Due to their high energy demands infant birds require feedings as often as every 15 minutes!

During the entire year, many birds are in need of assistance due to collisions with windows or being caught by cats.

Redhead

Wood Ducks & Mallards

# Geese and Ducks

In spring, Wildlife Haven admits hundreds of orphaned ducklings and goslings. Being very small in the wild without the protection of their parents, they risk being preyed upon. Since they are precocial birds, they don't require assistance from their parents to get nutrition and can self-feed. At our Centre, they are provided a large room, with small pools and other members of their own species. Once they are large enough they are released together into the wild.

- Precocial: young animals which are born/hatched with their eyes and ears open and are able to stand and walk, immediately upon birth/hatching.

Canada Goose

Canada Geese

# Raptors

Wildlife Haven admits a large number of Raptors throughout the year that are often starving, dehydrated, sick or injured. Our Centre may need to care for these patients for many months or years while they regain their strength. However, quick recoveries can occur and the patient can be released shortly after arrival. Non-releasable Raptors with good temperaments may be placed in education or breeding programs.

Swainson's Hawk

Gyrfalcon

Merlin

Red-Tailed Hawk

# Did you know...

- The eyesight of a Hawk is 8x greater than humans
- The Peregrine Falcon is the fastest animal on earth, it dives at 320 km/h; almost triple the speed of a running Cheetah
- Raptors have three eyelids to protect their eyes; an upper, lower and the nictitating membrane
- The nictitating membrane is transparent and protects the eye from drying out during flight

Bald Eagle

# Snowy Owls

Snowy Owls and lemmings, a type of rodent, have a unique predator-prey relationship. Every 3-5 years there is a fluctuation in the lemming population up in northern Canada. When the lemming population falls, Snowy Owls move south in search of food.

During these years, wildlife rehabilitators answer numerous calls about Owls on the side of roads; they are often starving, dehydrated and may have broken bones. Throughout this period, Wildlife Haven has been known to get up to 20 Snowy Owls that require rehydration and nutrition before they can be released back to the wild.

# Eastern Screech-Owl

At the beginning of June, an Eastern Screech Owl arrived at our Centre. The Owl had some minor injuries and damage to its left eye, which healed after a few weeks, allowing it to be released at the end of June.

## Owl Fun Facts

- Female birds of prey are 25% larger than males
- Owls have asymmetrical ears that are located beside the eyes; one ear is lower than the other ear, allowing them to locate prey by sound alone
- Owl eyes are fixed and they have evolved to be able to rotate their head 270 degrees to compensate
- Owls have very soft feathers that allow them to have silent flight

# Turtles

Western Painted Turtles and Common Snapping Turtles are admitted to Wildlife Haven often due to cracked shells as a result of collisions with cars. In these cases, our Centre can secure the shell with braces and let it grow back together. This is a slow process, similar to healing broken bones. Other times, turtles are mistakenly brought into our Centre when they are found away from water and can be quickly released.

**Western Painted Turtle**

**Western Painted Turtle**

# Did you know...

- The temperature of the egg determines whether the turtle inside will become a male or a female
- Male Turtles front claws are longer than their back claws. Female Turtles are larger than males
- Painted Turtles hibernate in the winter
- Painted Turtles are omnivores; they eat meat and plants
- Snapping Turtles are carnivores; they only eat meat

**Common Snapping Turtle**

# Fun Facts

- As Turtles grow, their shell sheds in layers, similar to when your skin peels
- Painted Turtles have a sharp ridged "horny beak" instead of teeth to help them eat
- The Turtle's rib cage is attached to the inside of their shell
- The Snapping Turtle has long, thick, sharp claws that allow it to tear apart its food and to climb hills
- A Snapping Turtle's neck is quite long; about 1/2 the length of its shell, and it can quickly extend to catch prey
- Most Turtles are able to pull their head, tail and legs into their shell to protect themselves from predators

**Common Snapping Turtle**

**Common Snapping Turtles**

# Education Ambassadors

Wildlife Haven has many non-releasable wildlife ambassadors, such as Raptors, Amphibians, and Reptiles. The Centre's ambassadors play an important role in educating the public about wildlife. Each ambassador has a unique story to tell about why they are not able to return to the wild and how each and every person can play a key role in protecting the species that inhabit our backyard.

Bopper

Earl

Rico

Luna

Majestic

BW

Karl

Milan

Bardy

Chinook

R2

Sitka

# Red

Red, a female Red-tailed Hawk was found as an illegally kept pet in 1984. Conservation officers retrieved her and brought her to Wildlife Haven. Her feathers had been clipped and with time, the feathers should have grown back. However, the feathers on her left wing never did; they had been trimmed too short and were permanently damaged. Red was left unable to fly, and was therefore non-releasable.

As our Centre's first wildlife ambassador, Red traveled to numerous schools, personal care homes and events. Her role was to educate the public about wildlife, specifically how they are not meant to be pets.

Red passed away at the age of 33 in 2014, and is one of the oldest known captive Red-tailed Hawks.

# Fun Facts

- Red-tailed Hawks can spot a small mammal from 30 meters in the air, about the height of an 8-story building

- Red-tailed Hawks are easily noticed by their rusty red tail feathers, which start to develop when they are 3 years old

- The Red-tailed Hawk's screech is often used in western movies in place of the eagles bark

- The eyes of the Red-tailed Hawk start out yellow and slowly change to dark-brown as they age

# Kricket

Kricket is a female American Kestrel. She fell out of her nest in the spring of 2010. The individuals who found her as an orphan kept her for a period of time before bringing her to Wildlife Haven. Unfortunately, she became imprinted during this time and was unable to be released.

When she arrived at our Centre, she was very stubborn and refused to eat anything except for crickets and grasshoppers, which is how she got her name.

## Did you know...

- Imprinting: when baby animals do not develop the natural wild behaviours needed to survive and often look to humans for food

# Avro

Avro is a female Swainson's Hawk that was admitted to Wildlife Haven in 2011 at 7 months of age. She was hit by a car that resulted in trauma, causing her to have impaired vision in her left eye and the loss of her right eye.

She is a calm bird that loves to spread her wings in the warm sun.

# Fun Facts

- Swainson's Hawks migrate all the way to Argentina, South America where insects are their main food source

- Swainson's Hawks migrate in large groups called 'kettles'. These kettles can include over 10,000 birds and may include other migratory raptors such as Broad-winged Hawks

- Swainson's Hawks develop a brown 'bib' on their chest when they are 4 years old

- When perched, the wings of the Swainson's Hawk extend to the end of the tail or longer

# Max

Max is a male Great Horned Owl. In 2007, he was found on the ground as a nestling and then admitted to Wildlife Haven. Max had a slight fracture on one wing and had parasites in his ears.

His wing healed, however his hearing is permanently damaged. This inhibits his natural ability to hunt; therefore he could not be released.

# Fun Facts

- The feather patterns of Great Horned Owls allow them to stay camouflaged during the day, when they are sleeping in trees

# Jet

Jet is an American Crow who was rescued as a fledgling in 2010. At our Centre, he was treated for a broken wing. The wing healed, but remained crooked, severely limiting his ability to fly.

Jet has learned to mimic voices and he can say phrases like "Hello!", "Who's out there?" and laugh. He is even able to distinguish between different coloured objects.

# Did you know...

- Crows are highly intelligent and can solve complex puzzles to get a reward

- Some species of Crows can construct tools to get food

- Crows can recognize faces, and will caw and swoop at humans who have mistreated them

- Crows will drop nuts on the roads for cars to crack, wait until the light changes red and the cars to stop, before retrieving the shelled nuts

- A group of Crows is called a 'murder'

# Bruce

Bruce is a Western Hognose Snake. A person who kept him as an illegal pet surrendered him to Wildlife Haven in 2013. He is a threatened species in Manitoba and we all need to help keep his species wild and protected.

# Did you know...

- In Manitoba, Western Hognose Snakes can only be found near Spruce Woods Provincial Park
- Western Hognose Snakes have an upturned snout that they use to burrow in the sand or dirt
- When threatened, Hognose Snakes play dead by rolling onto their backs with their mouths open, and may emit a foul scent to convince predators that they are unsafe to eat

# Salamanders

Tigger, Roo and Eeyore arrived at our Centre because they were kept illegally as pets.

George was collected for research by a third party and after was given to Wildlife Haven for education.

George is an Eastern Tiger Salamander who is very curious and loves to eat his crickets.

George

Tigger and Roo are Barred Tiger Salamanders who are very laid-back and love to soak in their pools.

← Tigger

Roo →

Eeyore is a Blue-spotted Salamander that loves to play hide-and-seek and is very shy.

## Fun Facts

- If a Salamander loses its tail or a limb, it will regrow, a process called regeneration
- To deter predators from attacking their head, Blue-spotted Salamanders will wag their tail. This causes the predator to attack the tail instead of the head or body

Eeyore

Made in the USA
Charleston, SC
25 July 2016